BIBLE CONNECT THE DOTS

Vickie Save

Illustrated by Ken Save

BARBOUR BOOKS
An Imprint of Barbour Publishing, Inc.

© 2001 by Barbour Publishing, Inc.

ISBN 1-58660-232-2

Published by Barbour Books, an imprint of Barbour Publishing, Inc., P.O. Box 719, Uhrichsville, Ohio 44683
www.barbourbooks.com

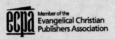 Member of the
Evangelical Christian
Publishers Association

Printed in the United States of America.
5 4 3

BIBLE
CONNECT
THE DOTS

ABRAHAM

WHO *WAS* ABRAHAM? WHY WAS THIS MAN SO IMPORTANT?

ABRAHAM WAS CALLED RIGHTEOUS. WHY? WAS HE A GOOD PERSON? DID HE ALWAYS DO WHAT WAS RIGHT? DID HE EVER DO SOMETHING WRONG WHEN HE WAS AFRAID? DID HE ALWAYS TRUST GOD? DID HE EVER TELL A LIE? DID HE EVER ASK ANOTHER TO TELL A LIE FOR HIM? WAS ABRAHAM CONSIDERED RIGHTEOUS BY HOW HE LIVED AND ACTED, OR BECAUSE HE BELIEVED GOD AND HIS PROMISES?

IN YOUR BIBLE, READ THE STORY OF ABRAHAM YOURSELF AND AS YOU READ THE VERSES THROUGH OUT THIS BOOK, LOOK FOR THE ANSWERS TO THESE QUESTIONS.

THEN ASK YOURSELF, *HOW DOES THIS STORY RELATE TO ME, MY LIFE, AND MY CHOICES TODAY? HOW DOES GOD VIEW ME AND WHAT I DO? WHO DO I BELIEVE: MYSELF, PEOPLE, OR GOD?*

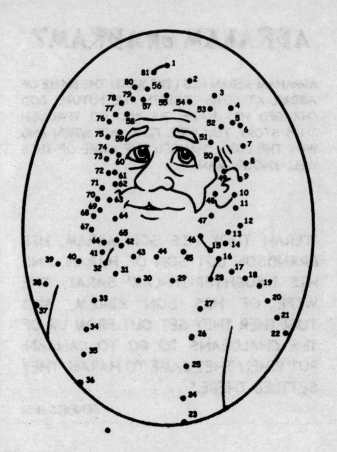

ABRAHAM or ABRAM?

ABRAHAM BEGAN HIS LIFE WITH THE NAME OF *ABRAM.* AT SOME TIME IN THE FUTURE, GOD CHANGED HIS NAME. AS YOU GO THROUGH THIS STORY, YOU WILL FIND OUT WHEN AND WHY THE LORD CHANGED THE NAME OF THIS WELL-KNOWN MAN.

"TERAH TOOK HIS SON ABRAM, HIS GRANDSON LOT SON OF HARAN, AND HIS DAUGHTER-IN-LAW SARAI, THE WIFE OF HIS SON ABRAM, AND TOGETHER THEY SET OUT FROM UR OF THE CHALDEANS TO GO TO CANAAN. BUT WHEN THEY CAME TO HARAN, THEY SETTLED THERE."

GENESIS 11:31

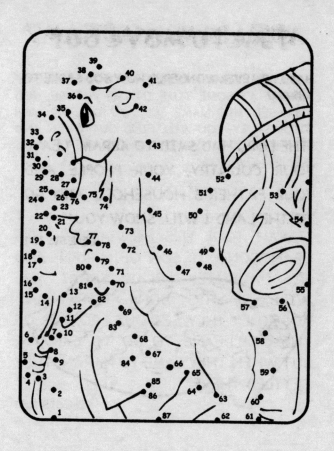

TIME TO MOVE OUT

HAVE YOU EVER WONDERED HOW GOD SPOKE TO ABRAM?

"THE LORD HAD SAID TO ABRAM, 'LEAVE YOUR COUNTRY, YOUR PEOPLE AND YOUR FATHER'S HOUSEHOLD AND GO TO THE LAND I WILL SHOW YOU.'"

GENESIS 12:1

I WILL BLESS YOU

WHY DO YOU THINK GOD CHOSE TO MAKE ABRAM INTO A GREAT NATION?

"'I WILL MAKE YOU INTO A GREAT NATION AND I WILL BLESS YOU; I WILL MAKE YOUR NAME GREAT, AND YOU WILL BE A BLESSING.'"

GENESIS 12:2

MORE BLESSINGS

WHY WILL ALL PEOPLE ON EARTH BE BLESSED THROUGH ABRAM?

"'I WILL BLESS THOSE WHO BLESS YOU, AND WHOEVER CURSES YOU I WILL CURSE; AND ALL PEOPLES ON EARTH WILL BE BLESSED THROUGH YOU.'"

GENESIS 12:3

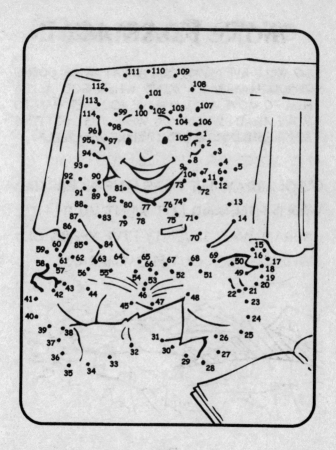

ON THE ROAD AGAIN

DO YOU EVER WONDER WHAT WAS GOING THROUGH ABRAM'S MIND WHEN GOD ASKED HIM TO MOVE AGAIN? HAVE YOU EVER HAD TO MOVE AGAIN WHEN YOU WERE JUST GETTING SETTLED IN? HOW DID IT MAKE *YOU* FEEL?

"SO ABRAM LEFT, AS THE LORD HAD TOLD HIM; AND LOT WENT WITH HIM. ABRAM WAS SEVENTY-FIVE YEARS OLD WHEN HE SET OUT FROM HARAN."

GENESIS 12:4

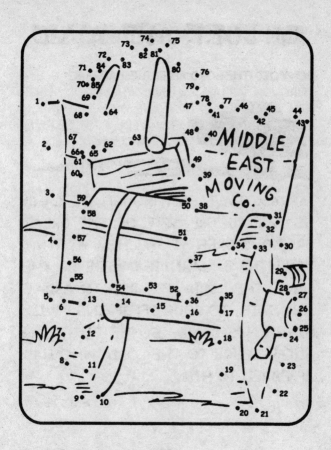

THE LORD APPEARED

HOW DID THE LORD APPEAR TO ABRAM?

"ABRAM TRAVELED THROUGH THE LAND AS FAR AS THE SITE OF THE GREAT TREE OF MOREH AT SHECHEM. AT THAT TIME THE CANAANITES WERE IN THE LAND. THE LORD APPEARED TO ABRAM AND SAID, 'TO YOUR OFFSPRING I WILL GIVE THIS LAND.' SO HE BUILT AN ALTAR THERE TO THE LORD, WHO HAD APPEARED TO HIM."

GENESIS 12:6–7

THINK, THINK, THINK

TERAH TOOK HIS SON, ABRAM, HIS GRANDSON,
LOT, AND, ABRAM'S WIFE, SARAI TO THE LAND
OF HARAN. JUST WHEN THEY WERE SETTLING
IN AND STARTING TO FEEL AT HOME, GOD
TOLD ABRAM TO LEAVE HIS COUNTRY AND HIS
FATHER'S HOUSEHOLD. GOD DIDN'T STOP
THERE! HE DIDN'T TELL ABRAM *WHERE* HE WAS
GOING. WHAT DID ABRAM DO ? HE DID AS GOD
ASKED HIM TO DO.

WHAT WOULD *YOU* HAVE DONE IF YOU WERE
ABRAM? WOULD YOU HAVE DONE WHAT GOD
ASKED YOU TO DO EVEN THOUGH YOU DIDN'T
KNOW WHERE YOU WERE GOING?

THINK, THINK, THINK!

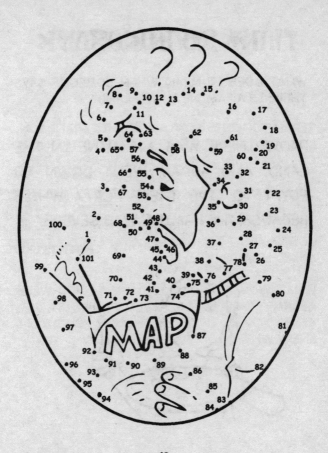

I'M SO HUNGRY!

WHAT DOES IT MEAN WHEN SOMEONE SAYS THERE IS A FAMINE IN THE LAND?

"NOW THERE WAS A FAMINE IN THE LAND, AND ABRAM WENT DOWN TO EGYPT TO LIVE THERE FOR A WHILE BECAUSE THE FAMINE WAS SEVERE."

GENESIS 12:10

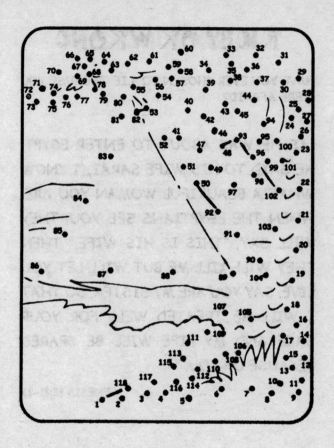

RIGHT OR WRONG

HAVE YOU EVER CHOSEN TO LIE BECAUSE YOU WERE AFRAID?

"AS HE WAS ABOUT TO ENTER EGYPT, HE SAID TO HIS WIFE SARAI, 'I KNOW WHAT A BEAUTIFUL WOMAN YOU ARE. WHEN THE EGYPTIANS SEE YOU, THEY WILL SAY, "THIS IS HIS WIFE." THEN THEY WILL KILL ME BUT WILL LET YOU LIVE. SAY YOU ARE MY SISTER, SO THAT I WILL BE TREATED WELL FOR YOUR SAKE AND MY LIFE WILL BE SPARED BECAUSE OF YOU.'"

GENESIS 12:11–13

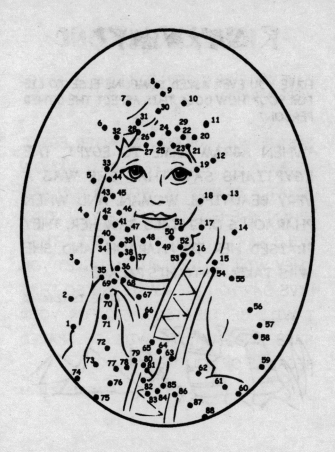

SAY WHAT?

HAVE YOU EVER ASKED SOMEONE ELSE TO LIE FOR YOU? HOW DOES THIS AFFECT THE OTHER PERSON?

"WHEN ABRAM CAME TO EGYPT, THE EGYPTIANS SAW THAT SHE WAS A VERY BEAUTIFUL WOMAN. AND WHEN PHARAOH'S OFFICIALS SAW HER, THEY PRAISED HER TO PHARAOH, AND SHE WAS TAKEN INTO HIS PALACE."

GENESIS 12:14–15

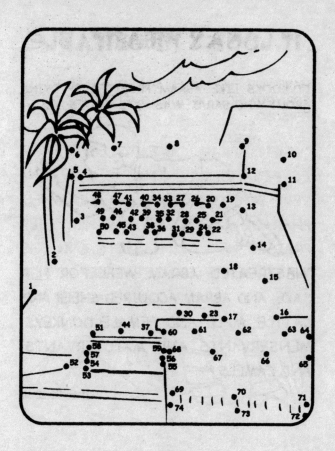

IT LOOKS PROFITABLE

IT LOOKS LIKE ABRAM PROFITED BY LYING ABOUT WHO SARAI WAS. BUT... *DOES* HE?

"HE TREATED ABRAM WELL FOR HER SAKE, AND ABRAM ACQUIRED SHEEP AND CATTLE, MALE AND FEMALE DONKEYS, MENSERVANTS AND MAIDSERVANTS, AND CAMELS."

GENESIS 12:16

27

YOU CAN'T LIE TO GOD

YOU MAY BE ABLE TO LIE TO PEOPLE BUT YOU CAN'T LIE TO GOD.

"BUT THE LORD INFLICTED SERIOUS DISEASES ON PHARAOH AND HIS HOUSEHOLD BECAUSE OF ABRAM'S WIFE SARAI."

GENESIS 12:17

THE TRUTH COMES OUT

HAVE YOU EVER THOUGHT THAT YOUR CHOICE TO LIE AND ASK ANOTHER TO LIE FOR YOU CAN CAUSE *ANOTHER* HARM?

"SO PHARAOH SUMMONED ABRAM. 'WHAT HAVE YOU DONE TO ME?' HE SAID. 'WHY DIDN'T YOU TELL ME SHE WAS YOUR WIFE? WHY DID YOU SAY, "SHE IS MY SISTER," SO THAT I TOOK HER TO BE MY WIFE? NOW THEN, HERE IS YOUR WIFE. TAKE HER AND GO!'"

GENESIS 12:18–19

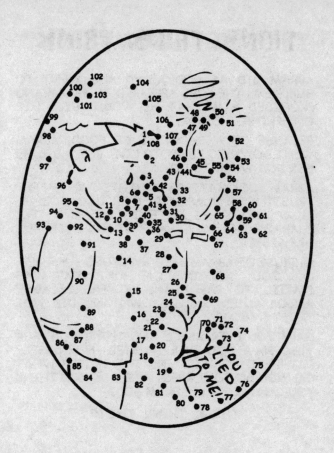

THINK, THINK, THINK

ABRAM DID AS GOD ASKED AND WENT TO SHECHEM. THE LORD APPEARED TO ABRAM AND PROMISED HIM THAT HE WOULD GIVE HIS OFFSPRING THE LAND.

BECAUSE OF A SHORTAGE OF FOOD, ABRAM WENT DOWN TO EGYPT TO LIVE. BUT. . .DID HE ASK *GOD* WHAT TO DO?

ABRAM TOOK MATTERS INTO HIS OWN HANDS, TRUSTING IN HIMSELF RATHER THAN GOD. HE ALSO ASKED HIS WIFE TO LIE AND TELL PHARAOH THAT SHE WAS NOT HIS WIFE, BUT HIS SISTER.

BECAUSE OF ABRAM'S LIE, EVERYONE SUFFERED. CAN YOU IMAGINE THE HURT THAT WAS CAUSED TO SARAI AND OTHERS BECAUSE ABRAM ACTED ON HIS OWN AND DID NOT TRUST IN GOD?

HAVE YOU EVER ASKED ANOTHER TO LIE FOR *YOU?* HAVE YOU EVER TRUSTED IN YOURSELF RATHER THAN GOD AND THE TRUTH? WHAT CAN YOU DO TO CORRECT A LIE? DO YOU THINK YOU CAN HIDE A LIE FROM GOD?

THINK, THINK, THINK!

33

PACKING AGAIN

ABRAM ONCE AGAIN PACKED UP HIS FAMILY AND HOUSEHOLD AND MOVED ON.

"SO ABRAM WENT UP FROM EGYPT TO THE NEGEV, WITH HIS WIFE AND EVERYTHING HE HAD, AND LOT WENT WITH HIM. ABRAM HAD BECOME VERY WEALTHY IN LIVESTOCK AND IN SILVER AND GOLD."

GENESIS 13:1-2

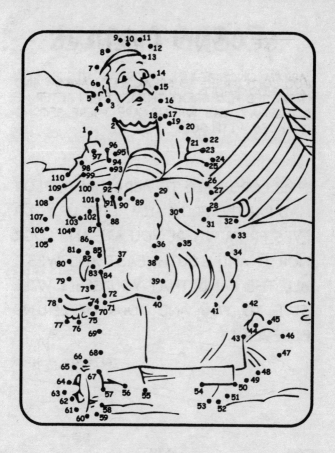

35

SECOND CHANCES

GOD CONTINUED TO SPEAK WITH ABRAM AND PROMISED HIM GREAT THINGS EVEN AFTER HE DID WHAT WAS WRONG. ARE THERE SECOND CHANCES WITH GOD?

"THE LORD SAID TO ABRAM AFTER LOT HAD PARTED FROM HIM, 'LIFT UP YOUR EYES FROM WHERE YOU ARE AND LOOK NORTH AND SOUTH, EAST AND WEST. ALL THE LAND THAT YOU SEE I WILL GIVE TO YOU AND YOUR OFFSPRING FOREVER.'"

GENESIS 13:14–15

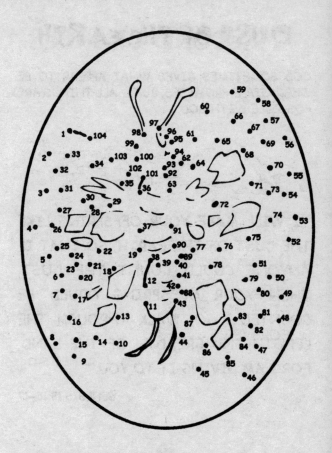

DUST OF THE EARTH

GOD SOMETIMES GIVES WHAT APPEAR TO BE *IMPOSSIBLE* PROMISES. BUT...ALL THINGS ARE POSSIBLE WITH GOD.

"'I WILL MAKE YOUR OFFSPRING LIKE THE DUST OF THE EARTH, SO THAT IF ANYONE COULD COUNT THE DUST, THEN YOUR OFFSPRING COULD BE COUNTED. GO, WALK THROUGH THE LENGTH AND BREADTH OF THE LAND, FOR I AM GIVING IT TO YOU.'"

GENESIS 13:16–17

PACKING YET AGAIN

WHY DID ABRAM BUILD AN ALTAR TO THE LORD? IS THIS ABRAM'S WAY OF REMEMBERING WHAT GOD HAS DONE FOR HIM AND HIS PROMISES TO HIM?

"SO ABRAM MOVED HIS TENTS AND WENT TO LIVE NEAR THE GREAT TREES OF MAMRE AT HEBRON, WHERE HE BUILT AN ALTAR TO THE LORD."

GENESIS 13:18

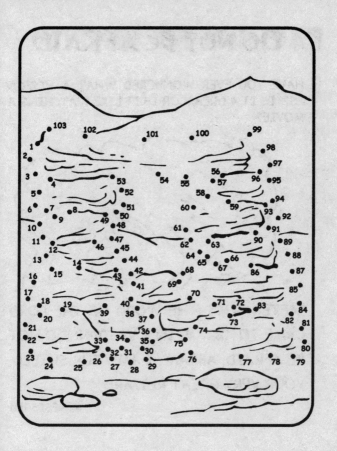

DO NOT BE AFRAID

HAVE YOU EVER WONDERED WHAT A *VISION* IS? IS IT A DREAM OR IS IT LIKE WATCHING A MOVIE?

"AFTER THIS, THE WORD OF THE LORD CAME TO ABRAM IN A VISION: 'DO NOT BE AFRAID, ABRAM. I AM YOUR SHIELD, YOUR VERY GREAT REWARD.'"

GENESIS 15:1

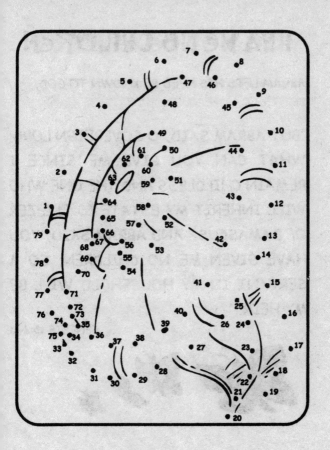

43

I HAVE NO CHILDREN

ABRAM LETS HIS NEED BE KNOWN TO GOD.

"BUT ABRAM SAID, 'O SOVEREIGN LORD, WHAT CAN YOU GIVE ME SINCE I REMAIN CHILDLESS AND THE ONE WHO WILL INHERIT MY ESTATE IS ELIEZER OF DAMASCUS?' AND ABRAM SAID, 'YOU HAVE GIVEN ME NO CHILDREN; SO A SERVANT IN MY HOUSEHOLD WILL BE MY HEIR.'"

GENESIS 15:2–3

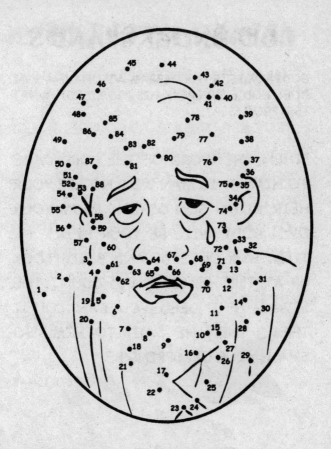

45

GOD UNDERSTANDS

GOD PROMISES THAT ABRAM WILL HAVE A SON.
DOES GOD EVER BREAK HIS PROMISES? WHAT
IS A PROMISE?

"THEN THE WORD OF THE LORD CAME
TO HIM: 'THIS MAN WILL NOT BE YOUR
HEIR, BUT A SON COMING FROM YOUR
OWN BODY WILL BE YOUR HEIR.' HE
TOOK HIM OUTSIDE AND SAID, 'LOOK
UP AT THE HEAVENS AND COUNT THE
STARS—IF INDEED YOU CAN COUNT
THEM.' THEN HE SAID TO HIM, 'SO
SHALL YOUR OFFSPRING BE.'"

GENESIS 15:4—5

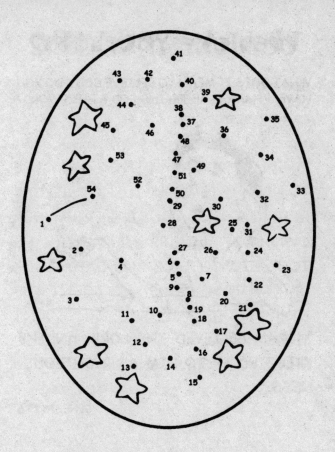

I BELIEVE YOU, LORD

WHAT DOES IT MEAN TO BELIEVE GOD? DO YOU HAVE A HARD TIME TAKING GOD AT HIS WORD?

"ABRAM BELIEVED THE LORD, AND HE CREDITED IT TO HIM AS RIGHTEOUSNESS."

GENESIS 15:6

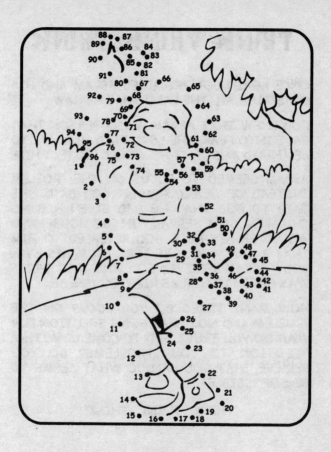

49

THINK, THINK, THINK

ONCE AGAIN GOD PROMISED ABRAM AND HIS OFFSPRING ALL THE LAND THAT HE SAW.

GOD KNEW THAT ABRAM WAS A PERSON THAT GAVE INTO FEAR. THE LORD TOLD HIM NOT TO BE AFRAID AND THAT *HE* WOULD PROTECT HIM.

ABRAM SEEMED TO FOCUS ON THE PROBLEM INSTEAD OF *HEARING* WHAT GOD SAID. HE SAID TO GOD THAT HE HAD GIVEN HIM NO CHILDREN, SO A SERVANT IN HIS HOUSEHOLD WOULD BE HIS HEIR. GOD REVEALED TO HIM THAT A SON WOULD BE BORN FROM HIS *OWN* BODY. ABRAM BELIEVED GOD, AND THIS BELIEF WAS GIVEN TO HIM AS RIGHTEOUSNESS.

HOW MANY TIMES DO YOU FOCUS ON THE PROBLEM AND NOT HEAR GOD'S SOLUTION FOR YOU? DO YOU TRUST GOD TO COME UP WITH A SOLUTION TO YOUR PROBLEMS? DO YOU BELIEVE THAT GOD CAN DO WHAT SEEMS TO BE IMPOSSIBLE?

THINK, THINK, THINK!

I AM THE LORD

WHY DO YOU THINK GOD TELLS ABRAM THAT HE IS THE LORD?

"HE ALSO SAID TO HIM, 'I AM THE LORD, WHO BROUGHT YOU OUT OF UR OF THE CHALDEANS TO GIVE YOU THIS LAND TO TAKE POSSESSION OF IT.'"

GENESIS 15:7

53

A COVENANT

WHAT DOES IT MEAN TO MAKE A COVENANT
WITH SOMEONE?

"ON THAT DAY THE LORD MADE A
COVENANT WITH ABRAM AND SAID, 'TO
YOUR DESCENDANTS I GIVE THIS LAND,
FROM THE RIVER OF EGYPT TO THE
GREAT RIVER, THE EUPHRATES—THE
LAND OF THE KENITES, KENIZZITES,
KADMONITES, HITTITES, PERIZZITES,
REPHAITES, AMORITES, CANAANITES,
GIRGASHITES AND JEBUSITES.'"

GENESIS 15:18-21

SARAI

IS THIS HOW GOD TOLD ABRAM HE WOULD HAVE CHILDREN?

"NOW SARAI, ABRAM'S WIFE, HAD BORNE HIM NO CHILDREN. BUT SHE HAD AN EGYPTIAN MAIDSERVANT NAMED HAGAR; SO SHE SAID TO ABRAM, 'THE LORD HAS KEPT ME FROM HAVING CHILDREN. GO, SLEEP WITH MY MAIDSERVANT; PERHAPS I CAN BUILD A FAMILY THROUGH HER.' ABRAM AGREED TO WHAT SARAI SAID."

GENESIS 16:1–2

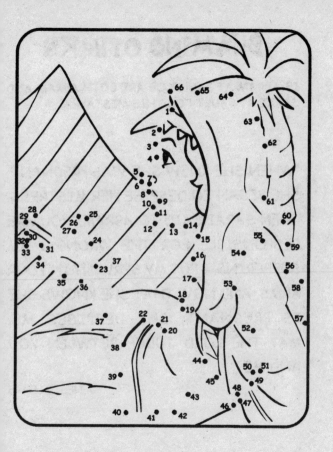

BLAMING OTHERS

IS ABRAM AT FAULT, OR ARE BOTH ABRAM AND SARAI AT FAULT FOR THIS MISTAKE?

"WHEN SHE KNEW SHE WAS PREGNANT, SHE BEGAN TO DESPISE HER MISTRESS. THEN SARAI SAID TO ABRAM, 'YOU ARE RESPONSIBLE FOR THE WRONG I AM SUFFERING. I PUT MY SERVANT IN YOUR ARMS, AND NOW THAT SHE KNOWS SHE IS PREGNANT, SHE DESPISES ME. MAY THE LORD JUDGE BETWEEN YOU AND ME.'"

GENESIS 16:4–5

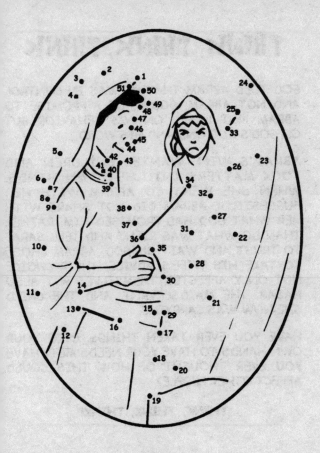

59

THINK, THINK, THINK

GOD TOLD ABRAM THAT HE WAS IN CONTROL AND NOT ABRAM. GOD MADE A PROMISE TO ABRAM NOT BASED ON *HIS* BEHAVIOR BUT ON GOD'S ACTIONS AND HIS WORD.

ABRAM'S WIFE WANTED CHILDREN AND TOOK MATTERS INTO HER OWN HANDS. WHEN SHE WENT TO ABRAM WITH HER SUGGESTION, ABRAM DID NOT SHARE WITH HER WHAT GOD HAD PROMISED HIM. RATHER THAN DO WHAT WAS RIGHT AND TELL SARAI TO TRUST AND WAIT ON GOD, ABRAM CHOSE TO TAKE HIS WIFE'S ADVICE. THEIR CHOICE NOT ONLY AFFECTED THEMSELVES BUT ALSO HAGAR, THE MAIDSERVANT, AND THE CHILD SHE NOW WAS CARRYING.

HAVE YOU EVER TAKEN THINGS INTO YOUR OWN HANDS TO HAVE YOUR NEEDS MET? HAVE YOU EVER THOUGHT OF HOW THIS COULD AFFECT OTHER PEOPLE?

THINK, THINK, THINK!

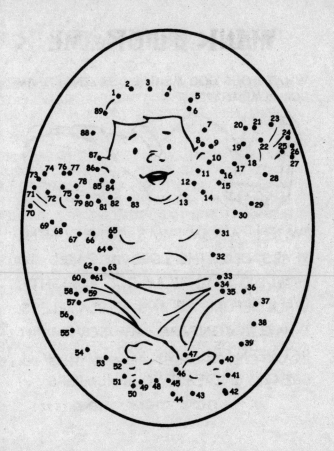

61

WALK BEFORE ME

WHAT DOES GOD MEAN BY SAYING, "I AM GOD ALMIGHTY?"

"WHEN ABRAM WAS NINETY-NINE YEARS OLD, THE LORD APPEARED TO HIM AND SAID, 'I AM GOD ALMIGHTY; WALK BEFORE ME AND BE BLAMELESS. I WILL CONFIRM MY COVENANT BETWEEN ME AND YOU AND WILL GREATLY INCREASE YOUR NUMBERS.'"

GENESIS 17:1–2

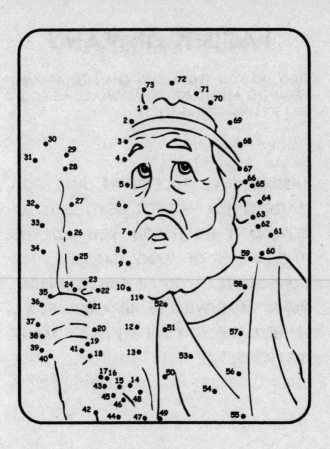

FATHER OF MANY

WHY DO YOU THINK GOD CHANGED ABRAM'S NAME TO ABRAHAM? WHAT WOULD BE GOD'S REASON FOR DOING THIS?

"ABRAM FELL FACEDOWN, AND GOD SAID TO HIM, 'AS FOR ME, THIS IS MY COVENANT WITH YOU: YOU WILL BE THE FATHER OF MANY NATIONS. NO LONGER WILL YOU BE CALLED ABRAM; YOUR NAME WILL BE ABRAHAM, FOR I HAVE MADE YOU A FATHER OF MANY NATIONS.'"

GENESIS 17:3-5

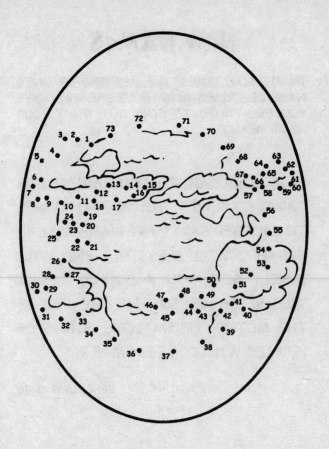

NEW NAMES

IN BIBLICAL TIMES, THE MEANING OF ONE'S NAME DESCRIBED *WHO* HE OR SHE WAS. HAVE YOU EVER TRIED TO FIND OUT WHAT YOUR NAME MEANS?

"GOD ALSO SAID TO ABRAHAM, 'AS FOR SARAI YOUR WIFE, YOU ARE NO LONGER TO CALL HER SARAI; HER NAME WILL BE SARAH. I WILL BLESS HER AND WILL SURELY GIVE YOU A SON BY HER. I WILL BLESS HER SO THAT SHE WILL BE THE MOTHER OF NATIONS; KINGS OF PEOPLES WILL COME FROM HER.'"

GENESIS 17:15–16

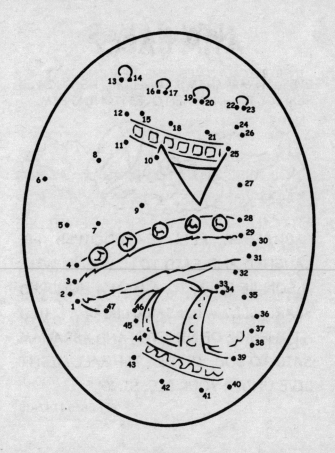

AT MY AGE?

EVEN IN ABRAHAM'S UNBELIEF, HE SHOWED RESPECT TO GOD WHEN QUESTIONING HIM.

"ABRAHAM FELL FACEDOWN; HE LAUGHED AND SAID TO HIMSELF, 'WILL A SON BE BORN TO A MAN A HUNDRED YEARS OLD? WILL SARAH BEAR A CHILD AT THE AGE OF NINETY?' AND ABRAHAM SAID TO GOD, 'IF ONLY ISHMAEL MIGHT LIVE UNDER YOUR BLESSING!'"

GENESIS 17:17–18

THINK, THINK, THINK

EVEN IN THE MIDST OF ABRAHAM'S MANY MISTAKES, GOD APPEARS AGAIN TO HIM AND CONFIRMS HIS PROMISE.

HE GIVES ABRAHAM A *NEW* NAME WHICH MEANS, "THE FATHER OF MANY NATIONS." GOD NOT ONLY GAVE ABRAHAM A NEW NAME BUT ALSO TOLD HIM *WHAT IT MEANS.* DO YOU THINK HE DID THIS SO THAT EVERY TIME ABRAHAM HEARD HIS NAME HE WOULD BE REMINDED OF GOD'S PROMISE OF A SON?

EVEN THOUGH ABRAHAM LAUGHED AND QUESTIONED GOD, HE SHOWED RESPECT WITH THE GESTURE OF FALLING FACEDOWN. HE KNEW THAT HE WAS JUST A MAN, BUT GOD WAS ALMIGHTY AND ALL POWERFUL.

DO YOU EVER QUESTION GOD AND HIS PROMISES TO YOU? HOW WOULD YOU QUESTION GOD WITH AN ATTITUDE OF RESPECT?

THINK, THINK, THINK!

ISAAC

GOD NOT ONLY PROMISED ABRAHAM A SON BUT NAMED HIS SON FOR HIM. I WONDER WHAT THE NAME ISAAC MEANS?

"THEN GOD SAID, 'YES, BUT YOUR WIFE SARAH WILL BEAR YOU A SON, AND YOU WILL CALL HIM ISAAC. I WILL ESTABLISH MY COVENANT WITH HIM AS AN EVERLASTING COVENANT FOR HIS DESCENDANTS AFTER HIM.'"

GENESIS 17:19

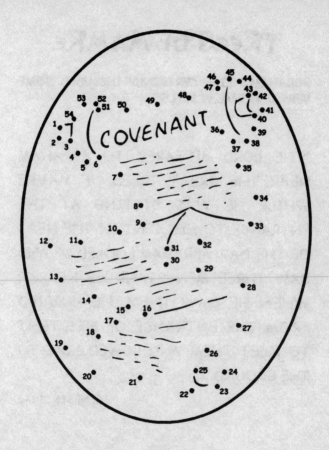

COVENANT

TREES OF MAMRE

ABRAHAM'S LIFE CERTAINLY INCLUDED SOME VERY UNUSUAL VISITORS!

"THE LORD APPEARED TO ABRAHAM NEAR THE GREAT TREES OF MAMRE WHILE HE WAS SITTING AT THE ENTRANCE TO HIS TENT IN THE HEAT OF THE DAY. ABRAHAM LOOKED UP AND SAW THREE MEN STANDING NEARBY. WHEN HE SAW THEM, HE HURRIED FROM THE ENTRANCE OF HIS TENT TO MEET THEM AND BOWED LOW TO THE GROUND."

GENESIS 18:1–2

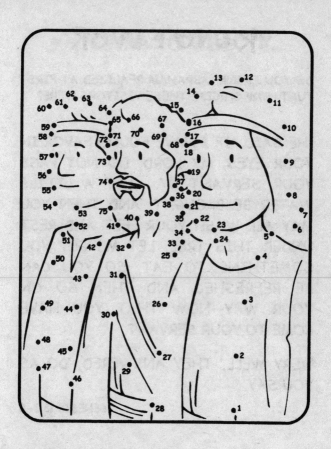

FOUND FAVOR

DO YOU THINK ABRAHAM REALIZED AT FIRST
JUST HOW SPECIAL THESE VISITORS WERE?

"HE SAID, 'IF I HAVE FOUND FAVOR IN
YOUR EYES, MY LORD, DO NOT PASS
YOUR SERVANT BY. LET A LITTLE
WATER BE BROUGHT, AND THEN YOU
MAY ALL WASH YOUR FEET AND REST
UNDER THIS TREE. LET ME GET YOU
SOMETHING TO EAT, SO YOU CAN
BE REFRESHED AND THEN GO ON
YOUR WAY—NOW THAT YOU HAVE
COME TO YOUR SERVANT.'

'VERY WELL,' THEY ANSWERED, 'DO AS
YOU SAY.'"

GENESIS 18:3—5

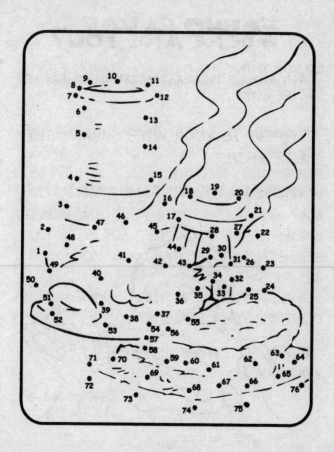

WHERE ARE YOU?

WHY WOULD THEY ASK ABRAHAM WHERE HIS WIFE WAS?

"'WHERE IS YOUR WIFE SARAH?' THEY ASKED HIM.

'THERE, IN THE TENT,' HE SAID."

GENESIS 18:9

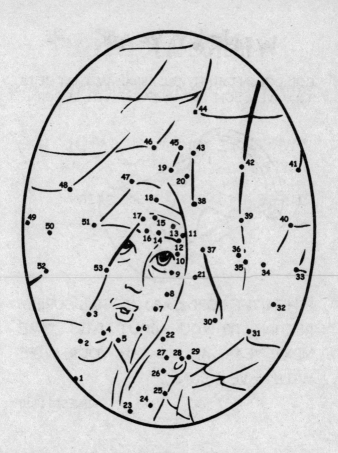

79

NeXt YeAr

GOD DOESN'T JUST TELL ABRAHAM THAT HE IS TO HAVE A SON, BUT *WHEN* HE WILL BE BORN.

"THEN THE LORD SAID, 'I WILL SURELY RETURN TO YOU ABOUT THIS TIME NEXT YEAR, AND SARAH YOUR WIFE WILL HAVE A SON.'"

GENESIS 18:10

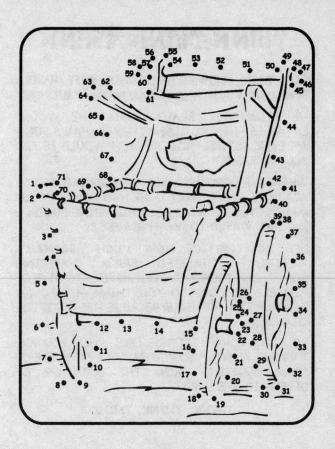

THINK, THINK, THINK

GOD TOLD ABRAHAM THAT HIS WIFE WOULD BEAR HIM A SON AND WOULD NAME HIM ISAAC.

HE PROMISED ABRAHAM THAT HE WOULD ESTABLISH HIS PROMISE WITH ABRAHAM'S SON— AN EVERLASTING PROMISE THAT WOULD BE FOR ALL HIS FAMILY.

WHEN THE LORD APPEARED TO ABRAHAM AGAIN, ABRAHAM ASKED THAT IF HE HAD FOUND FAVOR IN HIS EYES, HE WOULD LET HIM BRING FOOD TO EAT AND WATER TO WASH HIS FEET.

DID YOU NOTICE HOW MUCH ABRAHAM'S ATTITUDE CHANGED FROM WANTING SOMETHING FROM GOD TO WANTING TO GIVE OF HIMSELF TO GOD? DO YOU THINK GOD FOUND FAVOR WITH ABRAHAM BECAUSE HIS ATTITUDE CHANGED?

WHAT IS YOUR ATTITUDE LIKE WHEN YOU ARE TALKING TO GOD? DO YOU HAVE AN ATTITUDE OF ONLY WANTING FROM THE LORD OR OF GIVING TO THE LORD?

THINK, THINK, THINK!

83

WHEN I'M TIRED

DO YOU REALLY THINK THE LORD *DIDN'T* KNOW WHERE SARAH WAS, AND THAT SHE WAS LISTENING TO THEIR CONVERSATION?

NOW SARAH WAS LISTENING AT THE ENTRANCE TO THE TENT, WHICH WAS BEHIND HIM. ABRAHAM AND SARAH WERE ALREADY OLD AND WELL ADVANCED IN YEARS, AND SARAH WAS PAST THE AGE OF CHILDBEARING. SO SARAH LAUGHED TO HERSELF AS SHE THOUGHT, AFTER I AM WORN OUT AND MY MASTER IS OLD, WILL I NOW HAVE THIS PLEASURE?

GENESIS 18:10–12

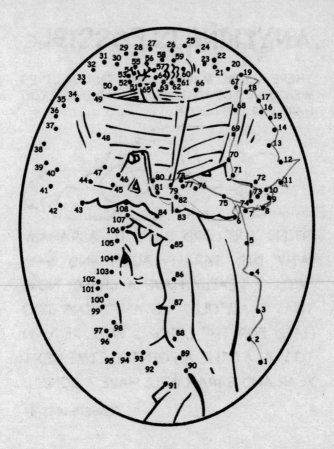

ANYTHING IS POSSIBLE

THERE ARE SO MANY THINGS IN OUR LIVES WE CANNOT CONTROL, BUT IS ANYTHING TOO HARD FOR THE *LORD*?

"THEN THE LORD SAID TO ABRAHAM, 'WHY DID SARAH LAUGH AND SAY, "WILL I REALLY HAVE A CHILD, NOW THAT I AM OLD?" IS ANYTHING TOO HARD FOR THE LORD? I WILL RETURN TO YOU AT THE APPOINTED TIME NEXT YEAR AND SARAH WILL HAVE A SON.'"

GENESIS 18:13–14

CHOOSING TO LIE

CAN YOU IMAGINE HOW *FOOLISH* IT IS TO LIE TO THE LORD?

"SARAH WAS AFRAID, SO SHE LIED AND SAID, 'I DID NOT LAUGH.'

BUT HE SAID, 'YES, YOU DID LAUGH.'"

GENESIS 18:15

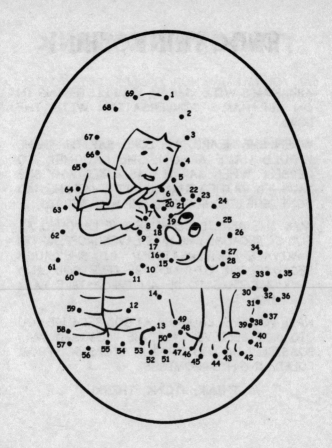

THINK, THINK, THINK

ABRAHAM'S WIFE, SARAH, WAS LISTENING IN ON ABRAHAM'S CONVERSATION WITH THE LORD.

WHEN SHE HEARD THE LORD SAY THAT SHE WOULD HAVE A SON, SHE LAUGHED TO HERSELF. WHEN SARAH WAS ASKED WHY SHE LAUGHED, RATHER THAN ADMIT WHAT SHE HAD DONE, SHE LIED BECAUSE SHE WAS AFRAID.

WAS SHE AFRAID BECAUSE SHE LAUGHED AT GOD OR BECAUSE SHE WAS EAVESDROPPING ON A PRIVATE CONVERSATION? DID SHE LAUGH BECAUSE SHE DID NOT BELIEVE GOD AND THOUGHT THIS TO BE AN IMPOSSIBLE TASK FOR HIM?

HAVE YOU EVER LAUGHED AT GOD BECAUSE YOU DID NOT BELIEVE WHAT HE PROMISED WAS POSSIBLE? DO YOU THINK IT STOPS GOD FROM FULFILLING HIS PROMISES?

THINK, THINK, THINK!

NOT AGAIN

ABRAHAM TRUSTS IN HIS *FEAR* ONCE AGAIN AND LETS THE KING BELIEVE SARAH IS HIS SISTER.

"NOW ABRAHAM MOVED ON FROM THERE INTO THE REGION OF THE NEGEV AND LIVED BETWEEN KADESH AND SHUR. FOR A WHILE HE STAYED IN GERAR, AND THERE ABRAHAM SAID OF HIS WIFE SARAH, 'SHE IS MY SISTER.' THEN ABIMELECH KING OF GERAR SENT FOR SARAH AND TOOK HER."

GENESIS 20:1-2

TIME TO MOVE AGAIN

93

SHE'S MARRIED

HOW DO YOU THINK THIS LIE AFFECTED ABIMELECH'S VIEW OF ABRAHAM?

"BUT GOD CAME TO ABIMELECH IN A DREAM ONE NIGHT AND SAID TO HIM, 'YOU ARE AS GOOD AS DEAD BECAUSE OF THE WOMAN YOU HAVE TAKEN; SHE IS A MARRIED WOMAN.'"

GENESIS 20:3

WHY?

HOW DO YOU DEAL WITH OTHER'S REACTIONS WHEN YOU HAVE DONE SOMETHING WRONG?

"THEN ABIMELECH CALLED ABRAHAM IN AND SAID, 'WHAT HAVE YOU DONE TO US? HOW HAVE I WRONGED YOU THAT YOU HAVE BROUGHT SUCH GREAT GUILT UPON ME AND MY KINGDOM? YOU HAVE DONE THINGS TO ME THAT SHOULD NOT BE DONE.' AND ABIMELECH ASKED ABRAHAM, 'WHAT WAS YOUR REASON FOR DOING THIS?'"

GENESIS 20:9–10

97

HALF-TRUTHS

PEOPLE HAVE A WAY OF TELLING THEMSELVES *ANYTHING* TO MAKE THEM FEEL BETTER.

"ABRAHAM REPLIED, 'I SAID TO MYSELF, "THERE IS SURELY NO FEAR OF GOD IN THIS PLACE, AND THEY WILL KILL ME BECAUSE OF MY WIFE." BESIDES, SHE REALLY IS MY SISTER, THE DAUGHTER OF MY FATHER THOUGH NOT OF MY MOTHER; AND SHE BECAME MY WIFE. AND WHEN GOD HAD ME WANDER FROM MY FATHER'S HOUSEHOLD, I SAID TO HER, "THIS IS HOW YOU CAN SHOW YOUR LOVE TO ME: EVERYWHERE WE GO, SAY OF ME, "HE IS MY BROTHER."'"

GENESIS 20:11–13

THINK, THINK, THINK

YOU WOULD THINK AFTER ALL THAT HAD HAPPENED, ABRAHAM WOULD TRUST *GOD* AND NOT GIVE INTO HIS FEAR!

ABRAHAM WAS ONLY HUMAN, AND THE FEAR WAS MORE POWERFUL TO HIM THAN TRUSTING GOD. AGAIN ABRAHAM TOOK MATTERS INTO HIS OWN HANDS.

THE KING, NOT ABLE TO UNDERSTAND WHY ABRAHAM WOULD DO SUCH A THING, QUESTIONED HIM. ABRAHAM ADMITTED HE DID IT OUT OF FEAR FOR HIMSELF AND TELLS THE KING SARAH WAS ONLY DOING WHAT HE HAD ASKED OF HER.

ABRAHAM USED A HALF-TRUTH TO PROTECT HIMSELF. A HALF-TRUTH IS WHEN PART OF THE STORY IS TRUE BUT YOU LEAVE OUT SOME. . .*IMPORTANT* DETAILS.

HAVE YOU EVER TOLD A "HALF-TRUTH" BECAUSE YOU WERE AFRAID? WERE YOU TRUSTING IN YOURSELF OR GOD BY TELLING HALF-TRUTHS?

THINK, THINK, THINK!

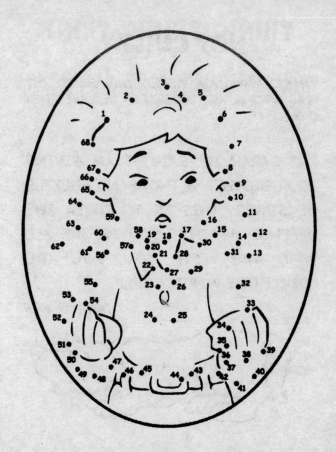

NOT GUILTY

WHAT ABRAHAM ASKED SARAH TO DO WAS WRONG, AND ABIMELECH DECLARED HER INNOCENT.

"TO SARAH HE SAID, 'I AM GIVING YOUR BROTHER A THOUSAND SHEKELS OF SILVER. THIS IS TO COVER THE OFFENSE AGAINST YOU BEFORE ALL WHO ARE WITH YOU; YOU ARE COMPLETELY VINDICATED.'"

GENESIS 20:16

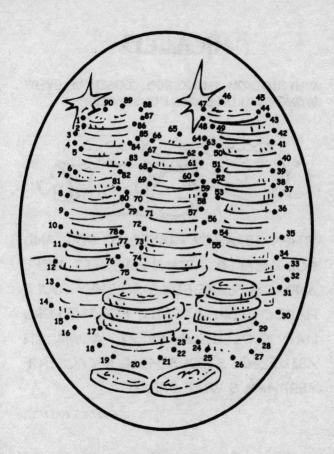

HEALED

WHY DO YOU THINK GOD CLOSED UP EVERY WOMB IN ABIMELECH'S HOUSEHOLD?

"THEN ABRAHAM PRAYED TO GOD, AND GOD HEALED ABIMELECH, HIS WIFE AND HIS SLAVE GIRLS SO THEY COULD HAVE CHILDREN AGAIN, FOR THE LORD HAD CLOSED UP EVERY WOMB IN ABIMELECH'S HOUSEHOLD BECAUSE OF ABRAHAM'S WIFE SARAH."

GENESIS 20:17–18

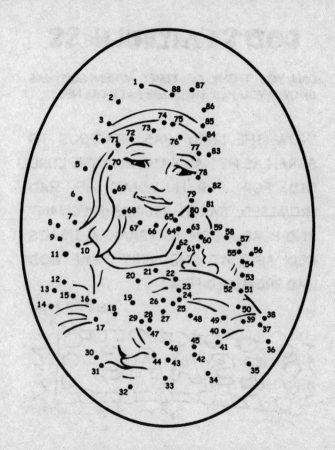

GOD'S FAITHFULNESS

CAN YOU THINK OF TIMES WHEN GOD HAS SHOWN YOU HIS AWESOME FAITHFULNESS?

"NOW THE LORD WAS GRACIOUS TO SARAH AS HE HAD SAID, AND THE LORD DID FOR SARAH WHAT HE HAD PROMISED. SARAH BECAME PREGNANT AND BORE A SON TO ABRAHAM IN HIS OLD AGE, AT THE VERY TIME GOD HAD PROMISED HIM."

GENESIS 21:1–2

THINK, THINK, THINK

ABIMELECH WENT TO SARAH AND TOLD HER THAT HE GAVE ABRAHAM A THOUSAND SHEKELS OF SILVER TO COVER THE OFFENSE AGAINST HER. HE TOLD HER SHE WAS NOT GUILTY OF ANY WRONG.

WHILE SARAH WAS IN ABIMELECH'S HOUSEHOLD, GOD STOPPED ANYONE FROM HAVING CHILDREN. ABRAHAM PRAYED TO GOD, AND GOD HEALED EVERY WOMB. ONCE ABRAHAM'S WRONG WAS CORRECTED, THE LORD DID FOR SARAH WHAT HE HAD PROMISED, AND SARAH BORE ABRAHAM A SON.

CAN YOU LEARN FROM ABRAHAM'S MISTAKE? HAVE YOU EVER DONE WRONG AND EXPECTED IN THE MIDST OF YOUR WRONG THAT GOD WOULD BLESS YOU?

IT TAKES COURAGE TO ADMIT TO YOUR WRONGS. EVEN THOUGH YOUR WRONGS DON'T CHANGE GOD'S PROMISES, HOW DO YOU THINK THEY STOP YOU FROM EXPERIENCING GOD'S PROMISES?

THINK, THINK, THINK!

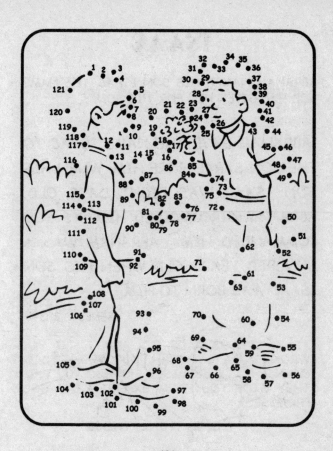

109

ISAAC

ABRAHAM NAMED HIS SON ISAAC, THE NAME GOD HAD GIVEN HIM FOR HIS SON.

"ABRAHAM GAVE THE NAME ISAAC TO THE SON SARAH BORE HIM. WHEN HIS SON ISAAC WAS EIGHT DAYS OLD, ABRAHAM CIRCUMCISED HIM, AS GOD COMMANDED HIM. ABRAHAM WAS A HUNDRED YEARS OLD WHEN HIS SON ISAAC WAS BORN TO HIM."

GENESIS 21:3-5

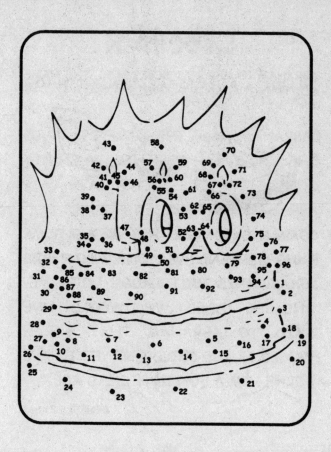

111

LAUGHTER

IMAGINE SARAH'S JOY AT GIVING BIRTH TO A SON IN HER OLD AGE!

"SARAH SAID, 'GOD HAS BROUGHT ME LAUGHTER, AND EVERYONE WHO HEARS ABOUT THIS WILL LAUGH WITH ME.' AND SHE ADDED, 'WHO WOULD HAVE SAID TO ABRAHAM THAT SARAH WOULD NURSE CHILDREN? YET I HAVE BORNE HIM A SON IN HIS OLD AGE.'"

GENESIS 21:6–7

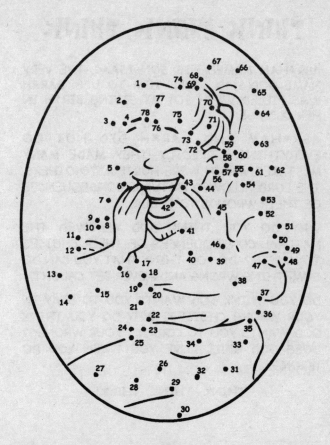

113

THINK, THINK, THINK

ABRAHAM NAMED HIS SON ISAAC, THE VERY NAME GOD HAD GIVEN HIM TO USE. SARAH WAS FILLED WITH JOY AT GIVING BIRTH IN HER OLD AGE.

ABRAHAM AND SARAH DID NOT DO EVERYTHING PERFECTLY—THEY MADE MANY MISTAKES WHICH WERE HURTFUL TO OTHERS. THE LORD ALLOWED NATURAL CONSEQUENCES OF THEIR WRONGS TO OCCUR.

WHY DO YOU THINK GOD ALLOWED THE NATURAL CONSEQUENCES OF THEIR CHOICES TO HAPPEN? DO YOU THINK THAT YOU CAN DO SOMETHING WRONG AND NEVER GET CAUGHT?

DO YOU THINK GOD WANTS YOU TO STAY IN YOUR WRONG CHOICES? WHY DO YOU THINK GOD WANTS YOU TO CORRECT YOUR WRONGS? DOES GOD STILL LOVE YOU WHEN YOU DO WRONG?

THINK, THINK, THINK!

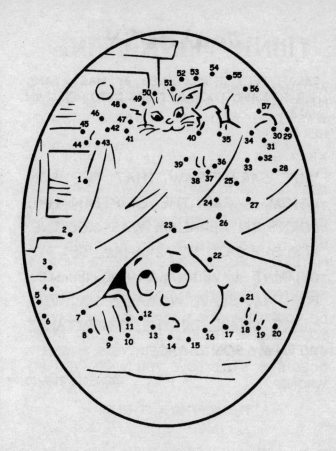

JEALOUSY

SARAH FELT THREATENED BY HAGAR AND
HER SON AND TOOK MATTERS INTO HER OWN
HANDS.

"BUT SARAH SAW THAT THE SON
WHOM HAGAR THE EGYPTIAN HAD
BORNE TO ABRAHAM WAS MOCKING,
AND SHE SAID TO ABRAHAM, 'GET RID
OF THAT SLAVE WOMAN AND HER SON,
FOR THAT SLAVE WOMAN'S SON WILL
NEVER SHARE IN THE INHERITANCE
WITH MY SON ISAAC.'"

GENESIS 21:9–10

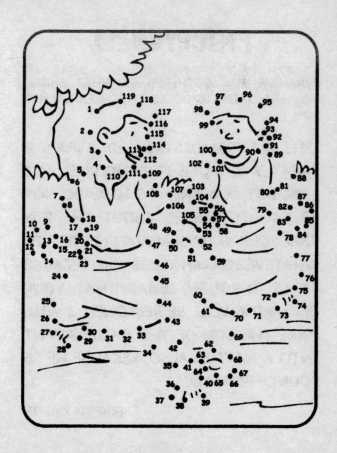

117

FRIGHTENED

ABRAHAM WAS BOTHERED BY WHAT SARAH HAD ASKED HIM TO DO AS IT CONCERNED HIS SON.

"THE MATTER DISTRESSED ABRAHAM GREATLY BECAUSE IT CONCERNED HIS SON. BUT GOD SAID TO HIM, 'DO NOT BE SO DISTRESSED ABOUT THE BOY AND YOUR MAIDSERVANT. LISTEN TO WHATEVER SARAH TELLS YOU, BECAUSE IT IS THROUGH ISAAC THAT YOUR OFFSPRING WILL BE RECKONED. I WILL MAKE THE SON OF THE MAIDSERVANT INTO A NATION ALSO, BECAUSE HE IS YOUR OFFSPRING.'"

GENESIS 21:11–13

HAGAR LEAVES

ABRAHAM TRUSTED THAT EVEN THOUGH HE DIDN'T LIKE SENDING HAGAR AWAY, GOD WOULD LOOK AFTER THEM BOTH AS HE HAD PROMISED.

"EARLY THE NEXT MORNING ABRAHAM TOOK SOME FOOD AND A SKIN OF WATER AND GAVE THEM TO HAGAR. HE SET THEM ON HER SHOULDERS AND THEN SENT HER OFF WITH THE BOY. SHE WENT ON HER WAY AND WANDERED IN THE DESERT OF BEERSHEBA."

GENESIS 21:14

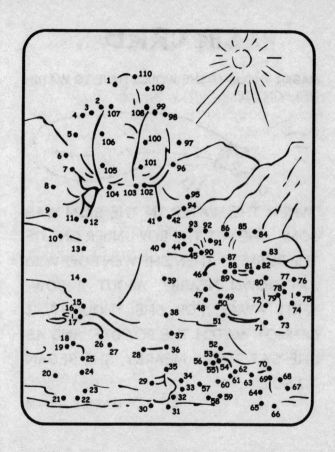

SHE CRIED

HAGAR THOUGHT SHE WOULD HAVE TO WATCH HER SON DIE.

"WHEN THE WATER IN THE SKIN WAS GONE, SHE PUT THE BOY UNDER ONE OF THE BUSHES. THEN SHE WENT OFF AND SAT DOWN NEARBY, ABOUT A BOW-SHOT AWAY, FOR SHE THOUGHT, 'I CANNOT WATCH THE BOY DIE.' AND AS SHE SAT THERE NEARBY, SHE BEGAN TO SOB."

GENESIS 21:15–16

FEAR NOT

GOD HEARD THE BOY CRYING AND PROMISED HAGAR HE WOULD TAKE CARE OF HIM.

"GOD HEARD THE BOY CRYING, AND THE ANGEL OF GOD CALLED TO HAGAR FROM HEAVEN AND SAID TO HER, 'WHAT IS THE MATTER, HAGAR? DO NOT BE AFRAID; GOD HAS HEARD THE BOY CRYING AS HE LIES THERE. LIFT THE BOY UP AND TAKE HIM BY THE HAND, FOR I WILL MAKE HIM INTO A GREAT NATION.'"

GENESIS 21:17–18

125

GOD PROVIDED

BECAUSE HAGAR WAS SO UPSET, SHE DID NOT SEE THE WELL UNTIL GOD OPENED HER EYES.

"THEN GOD OPENED HER EYES AND SHE SAW A WELL OF WATER. SO SHE WENT AND FILLED THE SKIN WITH WATER AND GAVE THE BOY A DRINK."

GENESIS 21:19

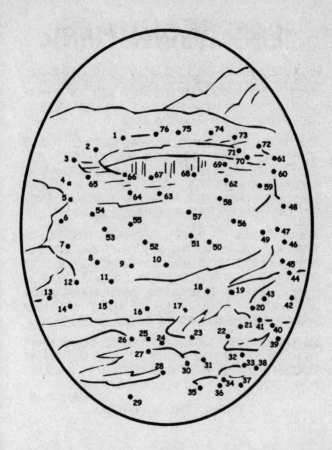

127

THINK, THINK, THINK

SARAH WAS JEALOUS OF HAGAR AND HER SON AND TOLD ABRAHAM TO GET RID OF THEM. GOD ASSURED HIM THAT HE WOULD EXTEND HIS PROMISE TO HAGAR'S SON.

WHEN HAGAR'S SUPPLIES HAD RUN OUT, SHE THOUGHT THAT THE BOY WOULD DIE, BUT GOD SPOKE WITH HER AND PROMISED THAT HE WOULD MAKE HER SON INTO A GREAT NATION. THEN GOD OPENED HAGAR'S EYES SO SHE COULD SEE THE WELL OF WATER.

MANY TIMES IN OUR LIVES WE WILL MAKE MISTAKES AND DO THINGS THAT ARE WRONG. GOD MAY NOT LIKE WHAT WE CHOOSE, BUT IT DOES NOT STOP HIM FROM LOVING US. GOD CAN USE OUR MISTAKES AND TURN THEM AROUND FOR GOOD WHEN WE ADMIT TO THEM AND TURN THEM OVER TO GOD.

IS THERE SOMETHING YOU HAVE DONE THAT IS WRONG? DO YOU THINK GOD CAN USE WHAT YOU HAVE DONE WRONG AND TURN IT AROUND FOR GOOD? WHAT DO YOU NEED TO DO?

THINK, THINK, THINK!

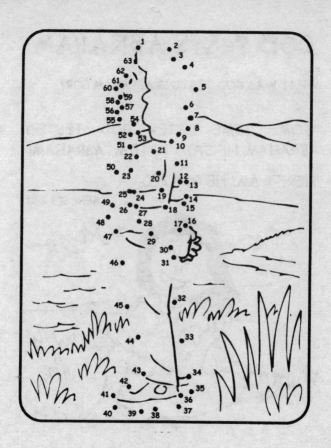

GOD TESTS ABRAHAM

WHAT WAS GOD TESTING ABRAHAM FOR?

"SOME TIME LATER GOD TESTED ABRAHAM. HE SAID TO HIM, 'ABRAHAM!'

'HERE I AM,' HE REPLIED."

GENESIS 22:1

EXCUSE ME, LORD?

DOES GOD REALLY GIVE YOU SOMETHING AND THEN TAKE IT AWAY?

"THEN GOD SAID, 'TAKE YOUR SON, YOUR ONLY SON, ISAAC, WHOM YOU LOVE, AND GO TO THE REGION OF MORIAH. SACRIFICE HIM THERE AS A BURNT OFFERING ON ONE OF THE MOUNTAINS I WILL TELL YOU ABOUT.'"

GENESIS 22:2

ALL RIGHT, LORD

COULD YOU IMAGINE WHAT ABRAHAM MUST HAVE BEEN FEELING EVEN THOUGH HE KNEW HE WAS DOING GOD'S WILL?

"EARLY THE NEXT MORNING ABRAHAM GOT UP AND SADDLED HIS DONKEY. HE TOOK WITH HIM TWO OF HIS SERVANTS AND HIS SON ISAAC. WHEN HE HAD CUT ENOUGH WOOD FOR THE BURNT OFFERING, HE SET OUT FOR THE PLACE GOD HAD TOLD HIM ABOUT."

GENESIS 22:3

135

WE WILL COME BACK

LOOK CAREFULLY AT WHAT ABRAHAM SAID. HE DID NOT SAY, "I WILL COME BACK," BUT "*WE WILL COME BACK.*"

"ON THE THIRD DAY ABRAHAM LOOKED UP AND SAW THE PLACE IN THE DISTANCE. HE SAID TO HIS SERVANTS, 'STAY HERE WITH THE DONKEY WHILE I AND THE BOY GO OVER THERE. WE WILL WORSHIP AND THEN WE WILL COME BACK TO YOU.'"

GENESIS 22:4–5

FOLLOWING THROUGH

ABRAHAM WAS DOING AS GOD ASKED, IN SPITE OF WHAT HE MAY HAVE BEEN FEELING .

"ABRAHAM TOOK THE WOOD FOR THE BURNT OFFERING AND PLACED IT ON HIS SON ISAAC, AND HE HIMSELF CARRIED THE FIRE AND THE KNIFE."

GENESIS 22:6

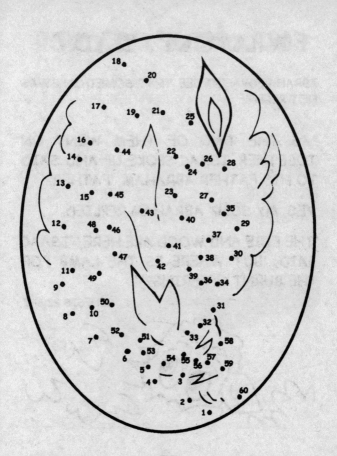

WHAT'S UP, DAD?

ISAAC BEGAN TO SEE THAT SOMETHING WAS NOT RIGHT.

"AS THE TWO OF THEM WENT ON TOGETHER, ISAAC SPOKE UP AND SAID TO HIS FATHER ABRAHAM, 'FATHER?'

'YES, MY SON?' ABRAHAM REPLIED.

'THE FIRE AND WOOD ARE HERE,' ISAAC SAID, 'BUT WHERE IS THE LAMB FOR THE BURNT OFFERING?'"

GENESIS 22:6-7

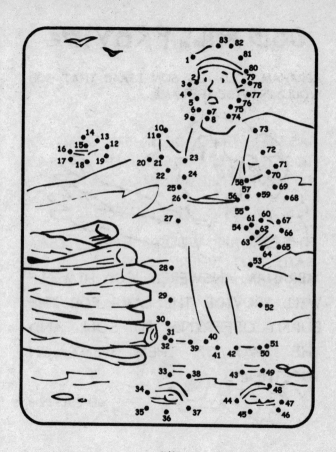

GOD WILL PROVIDE

ABRAHAM TOLD HIS SON ISAAC THAT GOD WOULD PROVIDE THE LAMB.

"ABRAHAM ANSWERED, 'GOD HIMSELF WILL PROVIDE THE LAMB FOR THE BURNT OFFERING, MY SON.' AND THE TWO OF THEM WENT ON TOGETHER."

GENESIS 22:8

143

ALL THE WAY

IT LOOKS LIKE GOD BROUGHT ABRAHAM RIGHT TO THE EDGE!

"WHEN THEY REACHED THE PLACE GOD HAD TOLD HIM ABOUT, ABRAHAM BUILT AN ALTAR THERE AND ARRANGED THE WOOD ON IT. HE BOUND HIS SON ISAAC AND LAID HIM ON THE ALTAR, ON TOP OF THE WOOD. THEN HE REACHED OUT HIS HAND AND TOOK THE KNIFE TO SLAY HIS SON."

GENESIS 22:9–10

THINK, THINK, THINK

GOD TESTED ABRAHAM, TELLING HIM TO
SACRIFICE HIS SON ISAAC. ABRAHAM DID NOT
TELL ANYONE ELSE ABOUT THIS—NOT EVEN
ISAAC.

ABRAHAM TOLD ISAAC THAT GOD WOULD
PROVIDE THE LAMB, BUT HE DID NOT SAY GOD
WOULD PROVIDE A SACRIFICE. ABRAHAM KNEW
WHAT GOD HAD PROMISED HIM ABOUT ISAAC.

CAN YOU IMAGINE WHAT BOTH ABRAHAM AND
ISAAC WERE FEELING AND THINKING DURING
THIS TIME? ABRAHAM TRUSTED IN GOD, AND
ISAAC TRUSTED IN HIS FATHER, ABRAHAM.

CAN YOU REMEMBER A TIME WHEN GOD TESTED
YOU? DID YOU DO AS GOD ASKED? WHAT WAS
THE SCARIEST PART FOR YOU?

THINK, THINK, THINK!

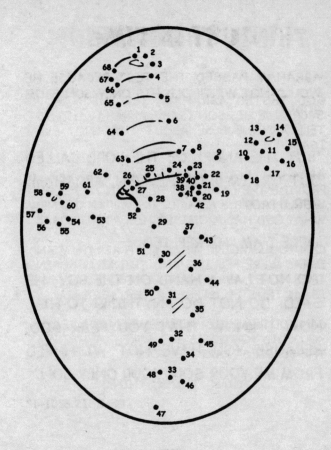

JUST IN TIME

ABRAHAM PASSED THE TEST BECAUSE HE WOULD NOT WITHHOLD HIS ONLY SON FROM GOD.

"BUT THE ANGEL OF THE LORD CALLED OUT TO HIM FROM HEAVEN, 'ABRAHAM! ABRAHAM!'

'HERE I AM,' HE REPLIED.

'DO NOT LAY A HAND ON THE BOY,' HE SAID. 'DO NOT DO ANYTHING TO HIM. NOW I KNOW THAT YOU FEAR GOD, BECAUSE YOU HAVE NOT WITHHELD FROM ME YOUR SON, YOUR ONLY SON.'"

GENESIS 22:11–12

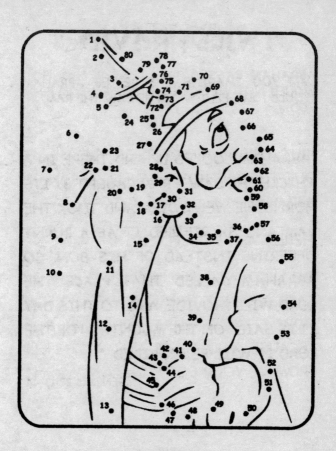

149

"I WILL PROVIDE"

CAN YOU IMAGINE THE RELIEF ABRAHAM WOULD HAVE FELT WHEN HE SAW THE RAM?

"ABRAHAM LOOKED UP AND THERE IN A THICKET HE SAW A RAM CAUGHT BY ITS HORNS. HE WENT OVER AND TOOK THE RAM AND SACRIFICED IT AS A BURNT OFFERING INSTEAD OF HIS SON. SO ABRAHAM CALLED THAT PLACE THE LORD WILL PROVIDE. AND TO THIS DAY IT IS SAID, 'ON THE MOUNTAIN OF THE LORD IT WILL BE PROVIDED.'"

GENESIS 22:13-14

ONE AND ONLY SON

WHAT COULD GOD MEAN WHEN HE SPOKE OF ALL NATIONS ON EARTH BEING BLESSED?

"THE ANGEL OF THE LORD CALLED TO ABRAHAM FROM HEAVEN A SECOND TIME AND SAID, 'I SWEAR BY MYSELF, DECLARES THE LORD, THAT BECAUSE YOU HAVE DONE THIS AND HAVE NOT WITHHELD YOUR SON, YOUR ONLY SON, I WILL SURELY BLESS YOU AND MAKE YOUR DESCENDANTS AS NUMEROUS AS THE STARS IN THE SKY AND AS THE SAND ON THE SEASHORE. YOUR DESCENDANTS WILL TAKE POSSESSION OF THE CITIES OF THEIR ENEMIES, AND THROUGH YOUR OFFSPRING ALL NATIONS ON EARTH WILL BE BLESSED, BECAUSE YOU HAVE OBEYED ME.'"

GENESIS 22:15–18

153

THINK, THINK, THINK

ABRAHAM WAS STOPPED BY GOD BEFORE ANY HARM CAME TO ISAAC. GOD KNEW BY ABRAHAM'S *ACTIONS* THAT HE PUT GOD FIRST, THAT HE TRUSTED IN GOD AND BELIEVED GOD AT HIS WORD.

GOD KNOWS EVERYTHING WE ARE THINKING AND FEELING. THERE IS NOTHING WE CAN HIDE FROM GOD. DID HE *NEED* TO HAVE ABRAHAM DO THIS TO PROVE HIS LOYALTY WHEN HE ALREADY KNEW ABRAHAM'S HEART? WAS THIS TEST FOR GOD OR WAS IT REALLY *FOR ABRAHAM?*

GOD KNEW THAT ABRAHAM NEEDED TO SEE FOR HIMSELF THAT HE LOVED GOD AND WOULD WITHHOLD NOTHING FROM HIM.

THROUGHOUT OUR LIVES, *WE* ARE GOING TO BE TESTED. THESE TESTS ARE NOT TO HARM US BUT TO HELP US GROW IN OUR FAITH AND TRUST IN GOD. IF GOD WERE TO ASK YOU TO SACRIFICE THE MOST IMPORTANT THING IN YOUR LIFE FOR HIM, WOULD YOU BE WILLING? WOULD YOU PASS THE TEST?

THINK, THINK, THINK!

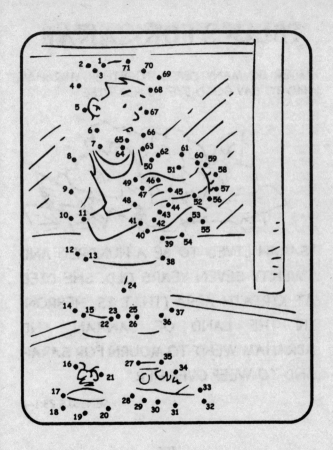

TEARS FOR SARAH

AFTER SO MANY YEARS TOGETHER, ABRAHAM HAD TO SAY GOOD-BYE TO HIS WIFE.

"SARAH LIVED TO BE A HUNDRED AND TWENTY-SEVEN YEARS OLD. SHE DIED AT KIRIATH ARBA (THAT IS, HEBRON) IN THE LAND OF CANAAN, AND ABRAHAM WENT TO MOURN FOR SARAH AND TO WEEP OVER HER."

GENESIS 23:1–2

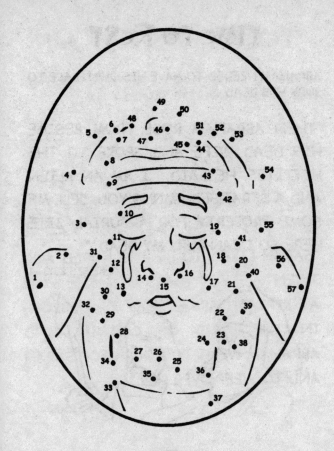

TIME TO REST

ABRAHAM NEEDED TO HAVE HIS OWN PLACE TO BURY HIS DEAD.

"THEN ABRAHAM ROSE FROM BESIDE HIS DEAD WIFE AND SPOKE TO THE HITTITES. HE SAID, 'I AM AN ALIEN AND A STRANGER AMONG YOU. SELL ME SOME PROPERTY FOR A BURIAL SITE HERE SO I CAN BURY MY DEAD.'"

GENESIS 23:3–4

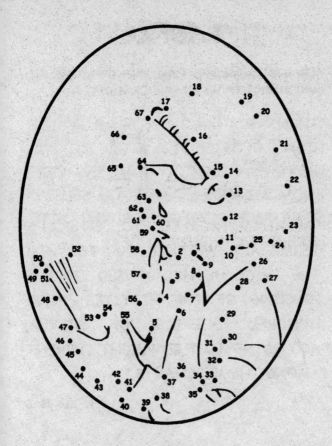

159

I AGREE

ABRAHAM HANDLED EVERYTHING FAIRLY AND ACCORDING TO WHAT EPHRON ASKED.

"ABRAHAM AGREED TO EPHRON'S TERMS AND WEIGHED OUT FOR HIM THE PRICE HE HAD NAMED IN THE HEARING OF THE HITTITES: FOUR HUNDRED SHEKELS OF SILVER, ACCORDING TO THE WEIGHT CURRENT AMONG THE MERCHANTS."

GENESIS 23:16

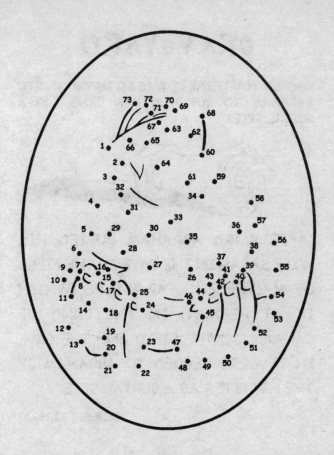

GRAVEYARD

WHY DO YOU THINK IT WAS SO IMPORTANT TO ABRAHAM TO BUY HIS OWN LAND FOR A BURIAL SITE?

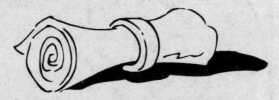

"AFTERWARD ABRAHAM BURIED HIS WIFE SARAH IN THE CAVE IN THE FIELD OF MACHPELAH NEAR MAMRE (WHICH IS AT HEBRON) IN THE LAND OF CANAAN. SO THE FIELD AND THE CAVE IN IT WERE DEEDED TO ABRAHAM BY THE HITTITES AS A BURIAL SITE."

GENESIS 23:19–20

THINK, THINK, THINK

ABRAHAM MADE MANY MISTAKES THROUGH-OUT HIS LIFE, BUT GOD'S PROMISE TO HIM NEVER CHANGED. GOD WAS ALWAYS FAITHFUL AND TRUE TO HIS WORD EVEN WHEN ABRAHAM WASN'T.

YOU CAN SEE THAT ABRAHAM STRUGGLED WITH FEAR. AFTER ISAAC WAS BORN AND GOD ASKED HIM TO SACRIFICE HIS ONLY SON, DO YOU SEE A DIFFERENT ABRAHAM? THROUGH HIS MISTAKES, MISTRUST, SELF-EFFORT, AND FEAR, ABRAHAM CAME TO KNOW NOT ONLY ABOUT HIS OWN HUMAN FRAILTIES BUT ALSO ABOUT GOD'S UNCONDITIONAL LOVE AND FAITHFULNESS.

ABRAHAM GREW UP AND LEARNED TO RELY AND TRUST IN GOD AND NOT HIMSELF.

WHEN YOU MAKE MISTAKES, DO YOU USE THEM TO GROW AND KNOW GOD THROUGH THEM? HOW CAN YOU USE YOUR MISTAKES TO GROW AND KNOW GOD?

THINK, THINK, THINK!

165

SWEAR BY THE LORD

ABRAHAM WANTED HIS SON TO HAVE A WIFE, BUT ONE FROM HIS OWN RELATIVES.

"ABRAHAM WAS NOW OLD AND WELL ADVANCED IN YEARS, AND THE LORD HAD BLESSED HIM IN EVERY WAY. HE SAID TO THE CHIEF SERVANT IN HIS HOUSEHOLD, THE ONE IN CHARGE OF ALL THAT HE HAD, 'PUT YOUR HAND UNDER MY THIGH. I WANT YOU TO SWEAR BY THE LORD, THE GOD OF HEAVEN AND THE GOD OF EARTH, THAT YOU WILL NOT GET A WIFE FOR MY SON FROM THE DAUGHTERS OF THE CANAANITES, AMONG WHOM I AM LIVING, BUT WILL GO TO MY COUNTRY AND MY OWN RELATIVES AND GET A WIFE FOR MY SON ISAAC.'"

GENESIS 24:1—4

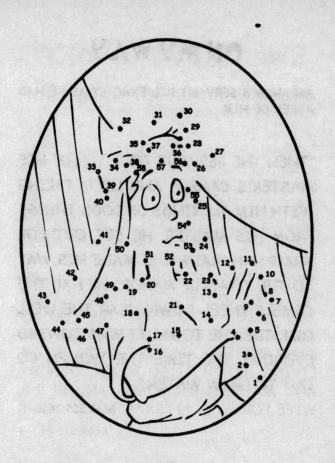

167

ON MY WAY

ABRAHAM'S SERVANT DID EXACTLY AS HE HAD ASKED OF HIM.

"THEN THE SERVANT TOOK TEN OF HIS MASTER'S CAMELS AND LEFT, TAKING WITH HIM ALL KINDS OF GOOD THINGS FROM HIS MASTER. HE SET OUT FOR ARAM NAHARAIM AND MADE HIS WAY TO THE TOWN OF NAHOR. HE HAD THE CAMELS KNEEL DOWN NEAR THE WELL OUTSIDE THE TOWN; IT WAS TOWARD EVENING, THE TIME THE WOMEN GO OUT TO DRAW WATER."

GENESIS 24:10–11

HELP ME, LORD

ABRAHAM'S SERVANT TURNED TO ABRAHAM'S GOD AND ASKED FOR HELP. WHY DO YOU THINK HE CALLED GOD, "ABRAHAM'S GOD"?

"THEN HE PRAYED, 'O LORD, GOD OF MY MASTER ABRAHAM, GIVE ME SUCCESS TODAY, AND SHOW KINDNESS TO MY MASTER ABRAHAM. SEE, I AM STANDING BESIDE THIS SPRING, AND THE DAUGHTERS OF THE TOWNSPEOPLE ARE COMING OUT TO DRAW WATER. MAY IT BE THAT WHEN I SAY TO A GIRL, "PLEASE LET DOWN YOUR JAR THAT I MAY HAVE A DRINK," AND SHE SAYS, "DRINK, AND I'LL WATER YOUR CAMELS TOO"—LET HER BE THE ONE YOU HAVE CHOSEN FOR YOUR SERVANT ISAAC. BY THIS I WILL KNOW THAT YOU HAVE SHOWN KINDNESS TO MY MASTER.'"

GENESIS 24:12–14

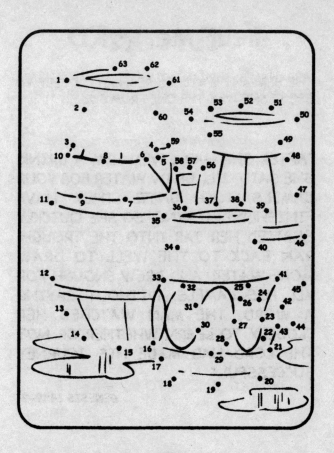

SUCCESS

THE SERVANT WATCHED REBEKAH CLOSELY TO SEE IF SHE WAS THE ONE FROM GOD.

"AFTER SHE HAD GIVEN HIM A DRINK, SHE SAID, 'I'LL DRAW WATER FOR YOUR CAMELS TOO, UNTIL THEY HAVE FINISHED DRINKING.' SO SHE QUICKLY EMPTIED HER JAR INTO THE TROUGH, RAN BACK TO THE WELL TO DRAW MORE WATER, AND DREW ENOUGH FOR ALL HIS CAMELS. WITHOUT SAYING A WORD, THE MAN WATCHED HER CLOSELY TO LEARN WHETHER OR NOT THE LORD HAD MADE HIS JOURNEY SUCCESSFUL."

GENESIS 24:19-21

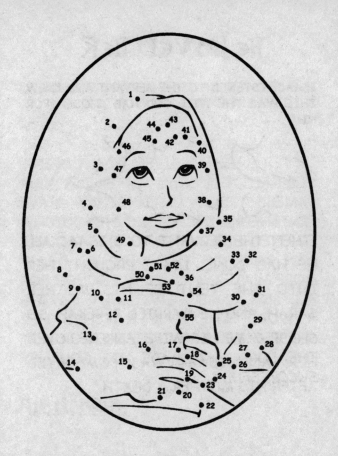

HE LOVED HER

ISAAC LISTENED TO THE SERVANT AND KNEW THIS WAS THE WIFE GOD HAD CHOSEN FOR HIM.

"THEN THE SERVANT TOLD ISAAC ALL HE HAD DONE. ISAAC BROUGHT HER INTO THE TENT OF HIS MOTHER SARAH, AND HE MARRIED REBEKAH. SO SHE BECAME HIS WIFE, AND HE LOVED HER; AND ISAAC WAS COMFORTED AFTER HIS MOTHER'S DEATH."

GENESIS 24:66–67

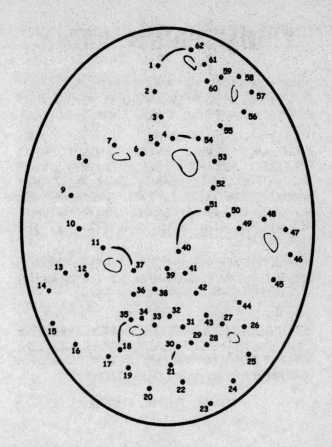

175

THINK, THINK, THINK

ABRAHAM KNEW HE WAS GETTING OLD, BUT BEFORE HE DIED HE WANTED TO KNOW THAT HIS SON ISAAC HAD A WIFE FROM THEIR OWN PEOPLE.

ABRAHAM'S SERVANT SWORE TO HIM TO DO AS HE ASKED. ABRAHAM'S SERVANT KNEW IN HIS MIND THAT THIS WAS A TASK THAT WAS *HUMANLY* IMPOSSIBLE. EVEN THOUGH HE DID NOT FOLLOW GOD HIMSELF, HE KNEW THAT ABRAHAM'S GOD WAS THE GOD OF THE IMPOSSIBLE.

HE PRAYED AND ASKED GOD TO HELP HIM. GOD DID JUST THAT, BRINGING TO THE SERVANT THE WIFE HE HAD CHOSEN FOR ISAAC.

IF SOMEONE WERE TO SEE *YOUR* RELATIONSHIP WITH GOD, WOULD HE SEE THAT YOU BELIEVE IN A GOD OF THE IMPOSSIBLE? DOES YOUR LIFE REFLECT GOD'S POWER AND LOVE OR YOUR *OWN* HUMAN EFFORTS AND LIMITATIONS?

THINK, THINK, THINK!

STARTING AGAIN

ONCE ABRAHAM HAD MADE SURE ISAAC WAS
TAKEN CARE OF, HE TOOK ANOTHER WIFE

"ABRAHAM TOOK ANOTHER WIFE,
WHOSE NAME WAS KETURAH. SHE
BORE HIM ZIMRAN, JOKSHAN, MEDAN,
MIDIAN, ISHBAK AND SHUAH."

GENESIS 25:1–2

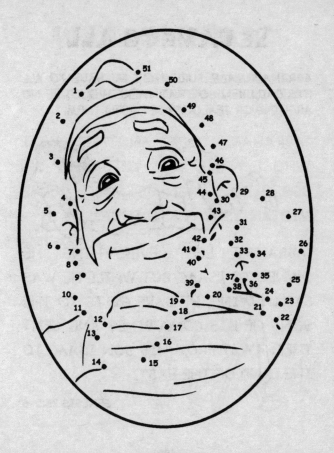

HE GAVE TO ALL

ABRAHAM MADE SURE THAT HE GAVE TO ALL HIS CHILDREN SO THAT THERE WOULD BE NO ARGUING OR JEALOUSY BETWEEN THEM.

"ABRAHAM LEFT EVERYTHING HE OWNED TO ISAAC. BUT WHILE HE WAS STILL LIVING, HE GAVE GIFTS TO THE SONS OF HIS CONCUBINES AND SENT THEM AWAY FROM HIS SON ISAAC TO THE LAND OF THE EAST."

GENESIS 25:5–6

MY TIME HAS COME

THE RECORD OF ABRAHAM'S LIFE TEACHES US SO MUCH. HIS LIFE IS FULL OF MANY EXPERIENCES THAT WE CAN LEARN FROM.

"ALTOGETHER, ABRAHAM LIVED A HUNDRED AND SEVENTY-FIVE YEARS. THEN ABRAHAM BREATHED HIS LAST AND DIED AT A GOOD OLD AGE, AN OLD MAN AND FULL OF YEARS; AND HE WAS GATHERED TO HIS PEOPLE."

GENESIS 25:7-8

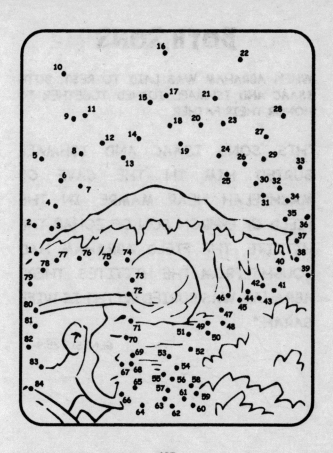

BOTH SONS

WHEN ABRAHAM WAS LAID TO REST, BOTH ISAAC AND ISHMAEL JOINED TOGETHER TO HONOR THEIR FATHER.

"HIS SONS ISAAC AND ISHMAEL BURIED HIM IN THE CAVE OF MACHPELAH NEAR MAMRE, IN THE FIELD OF EPHRON SON OF ZOHAR THE HITTITE, THE FIELD ABRAHAM HAD BOUGHT FROM THE HITTITES. THERE ABRAHAM WAS BURIED WITH HIS WIFE SARAH."

GENESIS 25:9–10

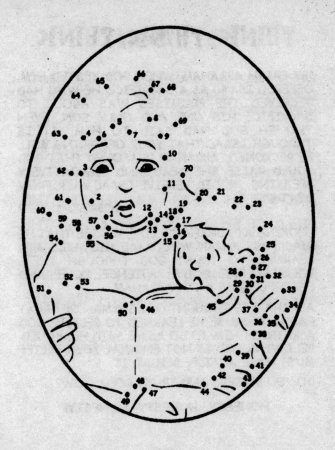

THINK, THINK, THINK

"BY FAITH ABRAHAM, WHEN GOD TESTED HIM, OFFERED ISAAC AS A SACRIFICE. HE WHO HAD RECEIVED THE PROMISES WAS ABOUT TO SACRIFICE HIS ONE AND ONLY SON, EVEN THOUGH GOD HAD SAID TO HIM, 'IT IS THROUGH ISAAC THAT YOUR OFFSPRING WILL BE RECKONED.' ABRAHAM REASONED THAT GOD COULD RAISE THE DEAD, AND FIGURATIVELY SPEAKING, HE DID RECEIVE ISAAC BACK FROM DEATH."

HEBREWS 11:17–19

LOOKING AT ABRAHAM'S LIFE, WE SEE THAT HE WAS JUST A MAN WHO MADE MISTAKES AND LEARNED TO TRUST GOD THROUGH THEM. WE ALSO SEE GOD'S PATIENCE, LOVE, AND FAITHFULNESS WITH ABRAHAM.

ABRAHAM IS THOUGHT OF AS A MAN OF GREAT FAITH BECAUSE HE LEARNED TO BELIEVE GOD AND TRUST HIM TO DO AS HE SAID HE WOULD. BELIEVING GOD IS NOT ENOUGH; YOUR BELIEF MUST HAVE *ACTION* BEHIND IT.

DO YOU BELIEVE AND TRUST GOD? HOW?

HONESTY, HONESTY, HONESTY!

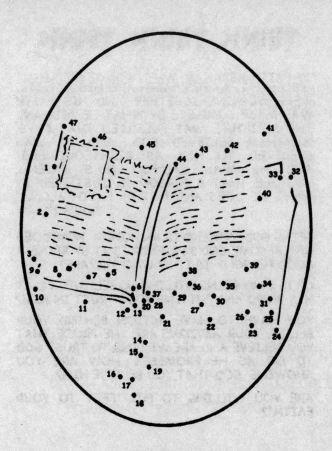

THINK, THINK, THINK

"YOU SEE THAT HIS FAITH AND HIS ACTIONS WERE WORKING TOGETHER, AND HIS FAITH WAS MADE COMPLETE BY WHAT HE DID. AND THE SCRIPTURE WAS FULFILLED THAT SAYS, 'ABRAHAM BELIEVED GOD, AND IT WAS CREDITED TO HIM AS RIGHTEOUSNESS,' AND HE WAS CALLED GOD'S FRIEND. YOU SEE THAT A PERSON IS JUSTIFIED BY WHAT HE DOES AND NOT BY FAITH ALONE."

JAMES 2:22–24

BEING GOD'S FRIEND IS AN HONOR. HOW DOES ONE BECOME GOD'S FRIEND? IS IT BY BEING A GOOD PERSON? IS IT BY WHO *YOU* ARE?

OR IS IT BY BEING WILLING TO BELIEVE GOD AT HIS WORD AND PUTTING YOUR TRUST IN *HIM*?

YOU HAVE TO HAVE ACTION BEHIND YOUR BELIEF. YOUR *ACTIONS* ARE THE PROOF THAT YOU BELIEVE AND ARE WILLING TO TRUST GOD TO DO AS HE PROMISES. HOW ARE YOU SHOWING GOD THAT YOU BELIEVE HIM?

ARE YOU WILLING TO PUT "FEET TO YOUR FAITH"?

JESUS

YOU'VE READ ABOUT A GREAT MAN WHO HAD A GREAT FAITH. BUT HOW DO *YOU* HAVE THAT KIND OF FAITH? DO YOU THINK YOU CAN HAVE THAT KIND OF FAITH? NOT BY YOUR OWN EFFORT—BUT THERE IS *ONE* WHO CAN DO IT THROUGH YOU! ASK JESUS AND HE WILL SHOW YOU HOW AS HE LIVES HIS LIFE IN YOU.

"LET US FIX OUR EYES ON JESUS, THE AUTHOR AND PERFECTER OF OUR FAITH, WHO FOR THE JOY SET BEFORE HIM ENDURED THE CROSS, SCORNING ITS SHAME, AND SAT DOWN AT THE RIGHT HAND OF THE THRONE OF GOD."

HEBREWS 12:2

IF YOU ENJOYED
BIBLE CONNECT THE DOTS,
Check out these other great Super Bible Activity books!

Bible Picture Fun
Coloring pages, "What's Wrong with This Scene?"
finish-the-picture, and more!

Amazing Mazes
Bible characters must navigate the
twists and turns of life.

Bible Scrambles
Unscramble Bible words to find the secret letters. . .
then unscramble the secret letters to solve the puzzle.

Each book: 192 pages, 4⅛" x 5⅜"

Available wherever books are sold.
Or order from:
Barbour Publishing, Inc.
P.O. Box 719
Uhrichsville, Ohio 44683
www.barbourbooks.com

**Only
$1.39!**

If you order by mail, please add $2.00 for shipping and handling.
Prices subject to change without notice.